SECRETS OF THE ANIMAL WORLD

CHAMELEONS
Masters of Disguise

by Eulalia García
Illustrated by Gabriel Casadevall and Ali Garousi

Gareth Stevens Publishing
MILWAUKEE

For a free color catalog describing Gareth Stevens' list of high-quality books and multimedia programs, call 1-800-542-2595 (USA) or 1-800-461-9120 (Canada). Gareth Stevens Publishing's Fax: (414) 225-0377.
See our catalog, too, on the World Wide Web: http://gsinc.com

The editor would like to extend special thanks to Jan W. Rafert, Curator of Primates and Small Mammals, Milwaukee County Zoo, Milwaukee, Wisconsin, for his kind and professional help with the information in this book.

Library of Congress Cataloging-in-Publication Data

García, Eulalia.
  [Camaleón. English]
  Chameleons: masters of disguise / by Eulalia García ; illustrated by Gabriel Casadevall and Ali Garousi.
    p. cm. – (Secrets of the animal world)
  Includes bibliographical references and index.
  Summary: Describes the physical characteristics, habitat, behavior, and camouflage technique of the lizard that can change color quickly to blend in with its environment.   .
  ISBN 0-8368-1647-1 (lib. bdg.)
  1. Chameleons–Juvenile literature. [1. Chameleons.] I. Casadevall, Gabriel, ill.
II. Garousi, Ali, ill. III. Title. IV. Series.
QL666.L23G3713 1997
597.95–dc21   97-8488

This North American edition first published in 1997 by
Gareth Stevens Publishing
1555 North RiverCenter Drive, Suite 201
Milwaukee, Wisconsin 53212 USA

This U.S. edition © 1997 by Gareth Stevens, Inc. Created with original © 1993 Ediciones Este, S.A., Barcelona, Spain. Additional end matter © 1997 by Gareth Stevens, Inc.

Series editor: Patricia Lantier-Sampon
Editorial assistants: Diane Laska, Rita Reitci

Printed in the United States of America

1 2 3 4 5 6 7 8 9 01 00 99 98 97

CONTENTS

THE CHAMELEON'S WORLD

Where chameleons live

Chameleons are creeping reptiles with scaly skin. Most of the eighty-five chameleon species are scattered over the African continent and Madagascar, living in humid forests or dry, desert areas. A few live in India and on islands in the Indian Ocean. One species lives in southern Europe.

Chameleons have three distinct features: a long tongue that moves quickly to catch prey, bulging eyes that can move independently of each other, and the ability to change skin color.

The chameleon has an extraordinary tongue with which it catches its basic diet — insects.

Most chameleon species live in Africa and Madagascar. Only one species inhabits Europe, in the southern part of the Iberian Peninsula.

Fascinating lizards

Chameleons are lizards that live in foliage. The digits on their limbs are divided into two sets opposite each other that help the animals grip tightly to branches. They can then remain motionless for hours at a time.

The chameleons' most fascinating feature is their ability to change color with incredible speed. Skin coloring is produced by pigments called chromatophores in some cells. Color

The chameleon's digits, joined in sets of two and three, form a useful tool to climb bushes and trees.

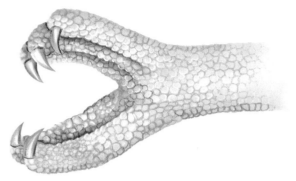

changes occur when pigments concentrate or disperse as a result of nervous impulses.

The chameleon's appearance is the result of adapting to its environment.

Masters of disguise

Earth's eighty-five chameleon species come in a variety of colors and sizes. Some are over 20 inches (50 centimeters) long. Others measure 2 inches (5 cm).

The Jackson's chameleon is about 5 inches (12 cm) long and lives in Africa. Males have three large horns, one above each eye and a third on the snout.

The flap-necked chameleon shows its dislike for rivals or enemies by raising one of the skin folds on the back of its head in disapproval.

The European species, the common chameleon,

JEWEL CHAMELEON

TWO-LINED CHAMELEON

DWARF CHAMELEON

COMMON
CHAMELEON

FLAP-NECK
CHAMELEON

JACKSON'S CHAMELEON

*The chameleon
species illustrated
here are among
the brightest and
most colorful.*

lives in dry places. In northern
Africa, it lives near desert oases.

The two-lined chameleon has
two light stripes that run along
its body. It also appears to wear
an armored helmet.

The jewel chameleon's dull
coloring camouflages it as it
rests, but, if disturbed, takes on
unusual, multicolored shapes.

The male dwarf chameleon
also takes on bright coloring
when it faces other males.

INSIDE THE CHAMELEON

The chameleon's most outstanding feature is its ability to change color according to the color of its surroundings. It is also a good climber with the help of its four clawed feet. Its long, sticky tongue traps its prey. The chameleon's slow, deliberate movements; its remarkable eyes; and its ability to change skin color all work to make it one of the world's most unusual reptiles.

LUNGS
The lungs are formed from many air sacs that increase the respiratory surface area. These sacs can blow themselves up to frighten rivals.

SKIN
Chameleons can change the color of their skin. Like some other reptiles, they can shed and sometimes eat the skin.

STOMACH

KIDNEYS

INTESTINE

TAIL
The tail is flexible and acts like a fifth limb. The skin on the underside has prickly scales that help it cling to branches.

HIND FEET
The hind feet have two sets of toes joined together by a membrane. Three toes point outward and two point inward.

HEAD
The head is like a helmet, sometimes with one or more horns. Chameleons use the horns to recognize each other and to show off during combat.

EYELIDS
The chameleon's eyes are large and bulging. Eyelids are round with a hole in the middle to let the iris show.

EYES
Chameleons move their eyes constantly, each one separately. They can see around them in a nearly complete circle.

TONGUE
When it spots an insect, the chameleon shoots out its tongue at lightning speed to catch its prey.

BRAIN

TRACHEA

TIP OF THE TONGUE
The reddish tip of the tongue is sticky and prehensile — very handy for catching prey.

ACCELERATOR MUSCLE
This special muscle helps the tongue shoot out to catch prey.

HEART

LIVER

SHOULDER
The chameleon's shoulder and hip joints are flexible and allow the animal to move easily from one branch to another.

BODY
The chameleon's compressed body makes it look like a leaf on a tree. This narrow body shape also helps it keep its balance better.

FOREFEET
Chameleons have five digits with strong claws arranged in two sets on each forefoot. Two of the fingers point outward and three point inward.

CONSTANTLY CHANGING

Chameleon colors

Skin color depends on pigment-bearing cells called chromatophores. Melanophores are the most common chromatophores. They contain melanin, a dark brown pigment. This pigment colors the skin different shades of brown. In humans, melanophores produce more pigment when exposed to the sun, causing a suntan. The melanophores have long arms that form part of the cells which make up the epidermis. Melanin is distributed along these arms and across the skin surface.

Chameleons also have other chromatophores with red and yellow pigments.

Light impulses enter the chameleon's eyes and go to the brain. The brain sends signals to the melanophores to dilate or concentrate the pigment.

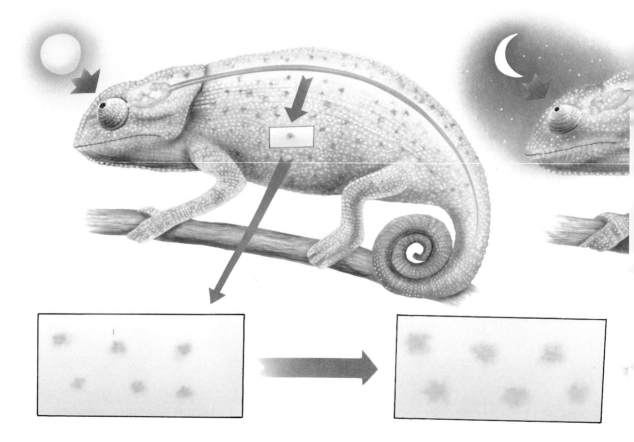

In some chameleons the brightly colored side stripes are typical, but they can disappear quickly.

Color changes occur because pigments move around inside the chromatophores. The chameleon's skin color is a result of the combination of different chromatophores and the degree of pigment dispersion. When a brown pigment spreads through an entire cell, the animal appears darker. When the pigment is concentrated in one part of the cell, the animal becomes paler. Red and yellow chromatophores work the same way.

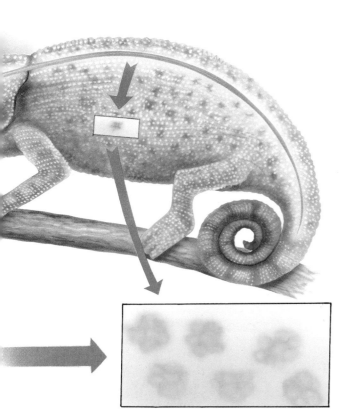

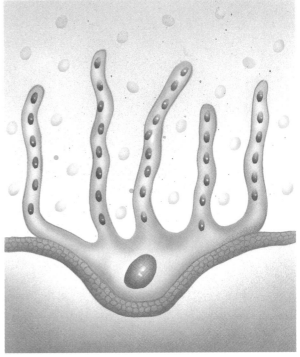

Melanophores stretch their arms to color the skin with melanin.

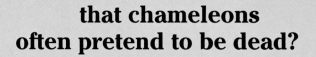

that chameleons
often pretend to be dead?

The chameleons' natural enemies are snakes and some birds. When a predator discovers them, chameleons often pretend to be dead because they cannot run quickly. Instead, the chameleons keep very still, with the eyes partly open. Since many predators prefer a freshly killed meal, this trick seems to work. Predators usually lose interest and move on.

Hide-and-seek

Most chameleons are homo-chromatic. They can turn green to blend in with foliage, or brown to blend in with tree bark.

African forest chameleons look like leaves with their curved back and sides and thin legs. They seem to be blowing in the wind as they move slowly back and forth. These chameleons have a subtle coloring, although males have rows of red growths on the head. Females are more uniform in color and are larger than the males.

Above: A chameleon skillfully camouflages itself by adopting the colors of its immediate surroundings.

Right: This small chameleon is well camouflaged by its subtle coloring, which blends in with the branches.

CAMOUFLAGE STRATEGY

The chameleon can perceive changes of light and background coloring as it searches for prey.

Changing disguises

In order to change color, the chameleon must be able to notice changes in its surroundings. With its eyes, it can perceive these changes and set off color changes. The skin is also able to produce color

A chameleon's skin is very sensitive. If a leaf casts a shadow on the chameleon, its silhouette will appear on the animal's skin.

changes according to the amount of light it receives.

If a leaf falls on a chameleon's skin and remains there for a while, the pale shape of a leaf will appear on the chameleon's skin. This happens because the chameleon's shaded skin is exposed to less light.

Temperature can also determine color changes. Chameleons get lighter as temperatures drop, and darker if temperatures go up.

Besides temperature and light, a chameleon's mood can also affect its color. If it is frightened or angry, it turns a darker color. When one male invades another's territory, it becomes brightly colored as a form of confrontation. When sick or dying, some chameleons turn a dull gray color.

A chameleon's camouflage is not always effective. It can be surprised and caught by an enemy.

that some chameleons
live on the ground?

The stump-tailed chameleon is only 3 inches (8 cm) long and lives among dead leaves and branches on the forest floors of East Africa.

This chameleon skillfully imitates the color of the dead leaves. Its brown coloring and rough-skinned body provide a perfect camouflage.

Like other chameleons, the stump-tailed chameleon moves slowly and can keep still for many hours, waiting for an insect lunch.

False chameleons

The chameleons and iguanas of the lizard family are best at changing skin color because of their chromatophores. One type of lizard, however, called the false chameleon, has unusually bright coloring in one part of its body, especially during the mating season.

In false chameleons, the bright green coloring is actually an optical illusion. Its pigment cells are full of crystals that disperse light.

This false chameleon's green color is only an optical illusion produced by the reflection of light on some of its skin cells.

Like the flash of a traffic light, this lizard unfurls a red sac under its throat to attract a mate.

Chameleon ancestors

Reptiles can survive in environments that are too poor for mammals and birds. This is because reptiles do not control their body temperature but depend on outside conditions. Mammals and birds need greater quantities of food to maintain a constant body temperature. A reptile can survive on less food than a mammal in the same adverse conditions.

Lizard ancestors appeared 250 million years ago. They were probably small reptiles that ate insects or dived under

This marine iguana is usually black, but in the mating season it changes color.

Some primitive lizards had long claws. Others were divers that swallowed stones to sink. They lived together with other reptiles that eventually evolved into mammals.

The frilled lizard is unusual. When alarmed, it unfolds a spectacular, brightly colored ruff to intimidate its rivals.

water to catch fish. The first chameleons evolved from primitive reptiles. Although there are few fossil remains, scientists know that a reptile similar to the chameleon — the Mimeosaurus — lived in Mongolia 130 million years ago.

Chameleons evolved from primitive forms into highly specialized animals. They are the only living reptiles that move as dinosaurs once did, with limbs that grow vertically down from the body. In most reptiles, the limbs grow sideways out of the body.

that chameleons
do not lose their tails
like other lizards?

Many lizards can lose their tails without suffering great harm. These parts break off easily and can usually grow back. Young lizards can grow their tails back to their original length. Older lizards usually grow back only a part of their tails. Chameleons do not have this ability. Their tails are too complex and valuable to lose, even though losing it could save their lives.

CHAMELEON BEHAVIOR

Slow-motion battles

During mating season, male chameleons fiercely defend their territories. When a male courts a female, it fights any other males that cross its path. To attract a female, a male assumes bright colors. Some species then place themselves where other males can easily spot them. When a rival appears and does not retreat, the two begin

Many male chameleons have large horns on their heads to use in battling for mates and for territory.

a slow battle of hissing, biting, and headbutting. The victor keeps the female and its own bright colors. The loser retreats, paler than at the beginning, a clear sign of defeat.

A male chameleon shows aggression toward another by blowing up its body and opening its mouth.

Born one year later

European chameleons mate in August. Two months later, the female digs out a tunnel in the ground. She stops digging long enough to sleep at night and starts again the next morning. When the tunnel is finished, she lays about thirty oval eggs and seals the entrance with dirt. She does not care for her babies.

Young chameleons keep their vitelline sac, their source of food in the egg, for three days after birth.

The young chameleons hatch about twelve months later. They measure about 2.4 inches (6 cm) and can already change color. At first, they are brown and light gray. Later, they adopt darker colors that help absorb heat.

Baby chameleons take about two hours to hatch.

Aim and . . . fire!

Chameleons can move their eyes separately, each eye seeing a different view. A chameleon can also point one eye forward and the other backward, then one upward and the other downward to search for food. When one eye sees an insect, the animal turns the other eye to help focus on its prey and calculate the distance. The animal shoots out its tongue in a fraction of a second. The insect sticks to the tip, and the chameleon slowly brings in its tongue and the food.

The chameleon's sticky, extendible tongue can measure as long as its body and head together.

With a lasso-like action, the chameleon's tongue hits its target and takes the insect to its huge mouth.

APPENDIX TO

CHAMELEONS
Masters of Disguise

CHAMELEON SECRETS

▼ **Sharp camouflage.** Many insects blend in incredibly well with their environments. This cricket looks like the thorns on the branches of its home.

▼ **Live births.** Most chameleons are oviparous, but some dwarf species give birth like mammals.

Internal buoys. Some chameleons use their lungs as buoys. If they accidentally fall into water, they float by blowing up their lungs.

▼ **Trunk birds.** Some birds are also good mimics. The tawny frogmouth, a bird similar to the nightjar, can imitate a tree trunk by keeping still for a long time.

Thirsty chameleons. Chameleons need to drink from time to time. Besides getting liquids from prey, chameleons drink morning dew.

Natural sunshade.
Chameleons bask in the sun for warmth. But too much heat is bad for them, and they hide among the foliage.

▼ Funny walk. Chameleons are not well adapted for walking on the ground. But many species can move quickly in a comical way.

1. Chameleons live mainly . . .
a) in India.
b) in South America.
c) in Africa and Madagascar.
d) in Australia.

2. When melanin disperses through an entire cell, an animal's skin . . .
a) pales.
b) does not change at all.
c) darkens.

3. A chameleon's skin turns dark when . . .
a) it is cold.
b) it is angry.
c) it is nighttime.
d) it is mating season.

4. How many species of chameleons are there?
a) Thirty.
b) Fifty.
c) Eighty-five.

5. Which chameleon has three prominent horns on its head?
a) The female Jackson's chameleon.
b) The male Jackson's chameleon.
c) No chameleon has horns.

6. What do chameleons do in times of danger?
a) They pretend to be dead.
b) They jump to the ground and run away as quickly as possible.
c) They allow their tails to break off.

The answers to CHAMELEON SECRETS questions are on page 32.

GLOSSARY

accelerator muscle: a muscle that speeds up an action.

adapt: to change behavior or adjust needs in order to survive in changing conditions.

adopt: to take on and use as one's own.

adverse: against or opposed to one's interests.

aggression: boldness; eagerness to challenge or enter combat.

ancestors: previous generations of a family or species.

assume: to take upon oneself.

buoy: an object that floats in water, usually to mark a position.

calculate: to judge or figure out; to solve the meaning of.

camouflage (v): to disguise something or someone to make it look like its surroundings. An animal's markings camouflage it so it blends into its background.

chromatophores: cells of an animal capable of causing skin color changes.

complex: complicated; made up of many parts or having many uses.

compressed: flattened, as if by pressure.

concentrate: to gather together into one body, force, or mass.

confront: to face or meet aggressively, as in an argument or fight.

court (v): to seek the affections or approval of another, especially a male of a female.

determine: to settle, decide, or fix; to bring about as a result.

digits: fingers and toes.

dilate: to become wide; to expand or swell up.

disperse: to distribute or spread widely.

effective: producing a desired result.

environment: the surroundings in which plants and animals live.

epidermis: the outer layer of skin.

expose: to be accessible to a particular action or influence.

extendible: capable of being stretched out to its full length.

flexible: able to bend or move with ease.

foliage: leaves and branches of plants, shrubs, and trees.

fossils: the remains of plants or animals from an earlier time period that are often found in rock or in Earth's crust.

fraction: a small part of.

homochromatic: of one color.

iguana: a type of large American lizard.

internal: within or inside.

intimidate: to make timid or fearful; to frighten.

invade: to enter by force or without permission.

mammals: warm-blooded animals that have backbones and hair. Female mammals produce milk to feed their young.

mate (v): to join together (animals) to produce young; to breed a male and a female.

melanophores: cells containing melanin, especially in fishes, reptiles, and amphibians.

membrane: a thin, soft, flexible layer of tissue in an animal or plant that lines or protects a certain part of its body.

optical illusion: a misleading image presented to the vision.

oviparous: able to produce eggs that hatch outside the mother's body.

perceive: to become aware of through the senses.

pigment: a substance in plants or animals that gives them color.

predators: animals that kill and eat other animals.

prehensile: adapted for seizing or grasping something.

prey: animals that are hunted and killed for food by other animals.

primitive: of or relating to an early and usually simple stage of development.

reptiles: cold-blooded, egg-laying animals with an internal skeleton and hornlike or scaly skin.

respiratory: referring to the act of breathing.

rivals: two or more individuals competing for food, territory, mates, or other advantage.

ruff: a fringe or frill of long hair, feathers, or skin growing on or around the neck.

silhouette: the outline of an object with no visible interior details.

snout: protruding nose and jaw of an animal.

spectacular: striking; sensational.

subtle: delicate, elusive, obscure.

territory: an area occupied by one or several of the same kind of animal that is used for foraging, and often includes nesting or denning locations.

vertically: upright; straight up and down.

vitelline sac: a membranous bag containing an egg yolk, which nourishes developing young.

ACTIVITIES

◆ Other animals besides chameleons are masters of camouflage. During a visit to a museum, or from library books and nature magazines, find as many different fish, birds, insects, amphibians, snakes, and lizards as you can that blend into their natural backgrounds. Which animals wear the same colors throughout their lives? Which have the ability to change their colors to match their backgrounds? What other kinds of markings do some animals wear that protect them from enemies?

◆ Do some research at the library and on the Internet to compile a list of the names of the eighty-five species of chameleons and where they live. Then draw a partial world map (like the one on page 4) to illustrate where the various chameleons can be found. Which species live in humid areas? Which species live in desert areas? Which chameleons are over 20 inches (50 cm) long? Which are about 2 inches (5 cm) long? What colors are they? What other features make each of the eighty-five species special and unique?

MORE BOOKS TO READ

Amazing Lizards. Trevor Smith (Knopf Books for Young Readers)
Animal Camouflage: A Closer Look. Joyce Powzyk (Simon & Schuster)
Black and White. Robyn Green and Bronwen Scarffe (SRA School Group)
Camouflage. Carolyn Otto (HarperCollins Childrens)
Chameleons. L. Martin (Rourke Corporation)
Chameleons. Peter Murray (Childs World)
Chameleons. Claudia Schnieper (Lerner Group)
Chameleons: Dragons in the Trees. James Martin (Crown Books)
Frillneck: An Australian Dragon. Pauline Reilly (Seven Hills Book)
Iguanas. L. Martin (Rourke Corporation)

VIDEOS

Camouflage, Cuttlefish, and Chameleons Changing Colors. (National Geographic)
Camouflage: How Animals Adapt to their Environment. (Wood Knapp)
The Chameleon. (International Film Bureau)
Chameleons. (New Dimension Media)
The World of Reptiles. (Kimbo Educational)

PLACES TO VISIT

St. Louis Zoological Park
Forest Park
Government Drive
St. Louis, MO 63110

Baltimore Zoo
Druid Hill Park
Baltimore, MD 21217

Granby Zoo
347 Bourget Street
Granby, Quebec J2G 1E8

Metropolitan Toronto Zoo
Meadowvale Road
West Hill
Toronto, Ontario
M1E 4R5

Royal Melbourne Zoological Gardens
Elliot Avenue
Parkville, Victoria
Australia 3052

Mugga Lane Zoo
RMB 5, Mugga Lane
Red Hill
Canberra, ACT
Australia 2609

Auckland Zoological Park
Motions Road
Western Springs
Auckland 2
New Zealand

INDEX

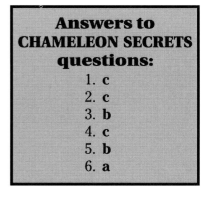

Answers to
CHAMELEON SECRETS
questions:
1. c
2. c
3. b
4. c
5. b
6. a